LEADING COUNSEL

LEADING COUNSEL

Spotlights on Top Elder Law and Estate Planning Attorneys

LEADING ELDER LAW AND ESTATE PLANNING ATTORNEYS

FEATURING:

Rebecca Auld

Nancy Hermansen

Matthew Yao

Melissa R. Victor

Amanda L. Smith

Samantha McCarthy

Wendy Mara

Sheri L. Montecalvo

Sharon Rutberg

Ted Alatsas

Remarkable Press™

The Global Autism Project 501(C)3 is a nonprofit organization that provides training to local individuals in evidence-based practice for individuals with autism.

The Global Autism Project believes that every child has the ability to learn, and their potential should not be limited by geographical bounds.

The Global Autism Project seeks to eliminate the disparity in service provision seen around the world by providing high-quality training to individuals providing services in their local community. This training is made sustainable through regular training trips and contiguous remote training.

You can learn more about the Global Autism Project and make direct donations by visiting **GlobalAutismProject.org**.

Leading Counsel/ Mark Imperial —1st ed.
Managing Editor/ Shannon Buritz

ISBN: 978-1-954757-07-3

CONTENTS

A NOTE TO THE READER

Thank you for obtaining your copy of "LEADING COUNSEL: Spotlights on Top Elder Law and Estate Planning Attorneys." This book was originally created as a series of live interviews; that's why it reads like a series of conversations, rather than a traditional book that talks at you.

My team and I have personally invited these Attorneys to share their knowledge because they have demonstrated that they are true advocates for the success of their clients and have shown their great ability to educate the public on the topic of Elder Law and Estate Planning.

I wanted you to feel as though the participants and I are talking with you, much like a close friend or relative, and felt that creating the material this way would make it easier for you to grasp the topics and put them to use quickly, rather than wading through hundreds of pages.

So relax, grab a pen and paper, take notes, and get ready to learn some fascinating insights from our Leading Counsel.

Warmest regards,

Mark Imperial
Publisher, Author, and Radio Personality

INTRODUCTION

"LEADING COUNSEL: Spotlights on Top Elder Law and Estate Planning Attorneys" is a collaborative book series featuring leading professionals from across the country.

Remarkable Press™ would like to extend a heartfelt thank you to all participants who took the time to submit their chapter and offer their support in becoming ambassadors for this project.

100% of the royalties from this book's retail sales will be donated to the Global Autism Project. Should you want to make a direct donation, visit their website at GlobalAutismProject.org

REBECCA
AULD

CONVERSATION WITH REBECCA AULD

> *Rebecca, you are an attorney with Auld Brothers Law Group based out of Pittsburgh, Pennsylvania. Tell us about your specialties and the people you serve.*

Rebecca Auld: An acquaintance once told me, "Every single adult individual needs your services." I hadn't ever really considered that. However, simply put, it is true. Everyone will need some help in their lifetime, as well as their family and friends. Often, clients look to the "now." It's a mindset of, "I don't have to worry about the stages of my life. I'm covered, as it's all tucked away in my safe." My point is that one tends to think of the "now" and not years down the road, with a different way of life.

It's not that simple, however. Within a Will and both Power-of-Attorneys, you're considering factors that you know. "I have three children and now five grandchildren." However, it's the moving parts that clients should consider. "What, Why, Where, When, and How?" are the questions I ask to get to know the client better. It's not and should not ever be about the attorney. It's a collaboration, discussing where you hope to be 10, 20, and 35 years from now.

I also practice in Estate Administration, Elder Law, Real Estate matters, Small Businesses, and Criminal Law. In the last area of law, no one wants to have to ask for my assistance. My practice focuses on listing and analyzing a client's different spheres of work, play, and future goals. They may look at each other but may intermingle typically at the time of passing. For instance, professionally, you own your business. Eventually, you either want to close your business, sell your business or have a family member act in your stead. So, what's your succession plan? Do you have one? If you have a business partner, what happens if one of you passes? After one passes away, those spheres consisting of your life typically merge. The merger can be a difficult road and a long one, at that.

Often I'm told, "I just need a simple Will and Power-of-Attorneys. Nothing complicated." Occasionally, I'll ask, "Do you think your life has been and is currently simple?" Kids vs. no kids, divorced, Medicaid might need to be applied for to include positive things, as well as retiring to your lakehouse in Colorado at 40.

As an Estate Planning Attorney, if you are not asking your clients for more information, you may not obtain all of the information that can be helpful. Everyone has different and unique situations. Do you have family members that can assist you? Do you have funds to sustain skilled nursing services? They are typically $10,000 a month for just room and board in Pittsburgh currently. That doesn't include medical or physical therapy costs, etc. Do you have the funds to pay privately?

One of the biggest questions I get is, "I want to protect my assets. Will they take my home? I've heard about this happening to other people. My friend told me that I need a Trust." A person can be fearful and wonder if they are doing the right thing. Clients are vulnerable by openly discussing private information, like a child or grandchild having a history of addiction. Lawyers are educators by assisting clients with options to make decisions best for them.

Do you find that many families are less than prepared for these situations? What specific concerns do your clients have?

Rebecca Auld: One client had a mother who outlived everyone's expectancy and lived in skilled nursing for 11 years. Long before, her son had moved home to help her. Unfortunately, she was not able to pay for her care privately. She had to apply for Medicaid, and at her passing, she had a significant amount of money that needed to be paid back. Her main asset was her home. Her son came to me and said, "I live in this home. I have been getting these documents from the government. I don't know what to do. Am I personally responsible for her debt? Will they take my home?" It's heartbreaking when an attorney has to walk a client through the process shortly after the parent has passed.

The majority of questions are about sheltering your wealth and avoiding Inheritance Tax, which not all states have, but Pennsylvania does at 0% to 15%. Pennsylvania does not have an Estate Tax, however. I suggest not moving to Maryland, as they have both. Adult children want to know what to do when their elderly parent(s) cannot live by themselves anymore. They are worried they will refuse. The law wants to be black and white, but it's a sea full of gray.

There is a lot of talk about power of attorney. Can you explain this role?

Rebecca Auld: Typically, clients are most worried about having their Wills drafted. These Wills are only legal when you pass away and are filed with the Court if Probate is needed. However, it's your Financial Power-of-Attorney and Healthcare Power-of-Attorneys that are most important. Eventually, everyone needs help. The usage of both can either be determined when your doctor(s) medically indicate you lack capacity OR once they are signed, they are active and usable.

Who likes HIPAA? HIPPA likes HIPPA. Even if you are married, it's a misnomer that you legally can take over bank accounts in your spouse's name, sign Tax Returns, sign Deeds, question bills, call doctor's offices, insurance companies, or financial institutions and make medical decisions. In Pennsylvania, at least, you're able to change things like beneficiaries on a life insurance policy to include your children if your spouse has passed, leaving no named beneficiary. During a person's lifetime, the taxable state wants to tax what's already been taxed previously. You've given them a lot of your hard-earned money. Why should they take more at death?

Regarding whom you should appoint as your Agent, clients are often fearful of giving someone the absolute power to handle all future financial and medical matters. If that's a worry, you may not be choosing the right person for the task. I use my parents as an example. My mother is a retired nurse enabling her to ask the right questions and is mentally capable of making those tough decisions. On the other hand, she can not be my Financial Power-of-Attorney, as it's not her forte. However, my father, a retired attorney who mainly handled Estate Administration and Estate Planning, can, as he knows the process well.

For each, you must make the right decision for yourself and not worry about upsetting family members. Save yourself and your family a significant amount of stress and aggravation. Estate Planning attorneys do not want to see a person's wishes and specific directives ignored. They certainly do not want to tell family and friends that due to the lack of Power-of-Attorneys, an individual in a black robe will make those decisions via a legal Guardian.

I end with the remark that I tell clients, "You're the boss. Make those decisions while you are able. What a full life you will have lived, as seen on paper, as it will be far from simple."

What inspired you to get started in elder law?

Rebecca Auld: I've always enjoyed helping people since grade school. Elder law isn't my only area of practice, simply because you're talking about one's personal life and professional life to include the needs of your immediate and extended family. I genuinely want to help people. I want clients to see things they may be worried about, consider the highs and lows seen or unseen, and work towards goals and a way of life they hope to achieve. I've, in essence, lived or will have lived hundreds of lives vicariously. I track families for generations helping their children and grandchildren to make the best-educated decisions they can for their benefit alone.

For me, it was either become a teacher or professor or practice law. Since I was done with paper writing and tests, I went in the direction of passing one big last and final test.

How can people find you and connect with you?

Rebecca Auld: I can be found in the Pittsburgh area. The firm's website is www.AuldBrothersLaw.com, serving

Allegheny and Butler County in Pennsylvania. Our phone number is (412) 487-8668. I can also be reached via email, which is Rauld@AuldBrothersLaw.com. Even if I can not assist you, I'm happy to point individuals in the right direction, if possible.

REBECCA A. AULD

Attorney-at-Law, Auld Brothers Law Group

Rebecca A. Auld is the principal at Auld Brothers Law Group. Her practice consists of; Wills, Financial and Healthcare Power-of-Attorneys, Estate Administration, Elder Law, Real Estate matters, Small Businesses, and Criminal Law.

She is a 2000 *cum laude* graduate of Denison University in Granville, Ohio. During college and from 2000-2003 at the Duquesne University School-of-Law, Rebecca interned and worked for the Office of the Attorney General, Commonwealth of Pennsylvania, under Mike Fisher. Additionally, she interned for the United States Attorney's Office of the Prosecutor for the United States District Court for the Eastern District of Pennsylvania.

Upon graduating from Duquesne, Rebecca clerked for the late Honorable George H. Hancher from 2003 to 2006, writing Opinions in the Court of Common Pleas of Butler County of Pennsylvania, where she came to understand fully and wholly respect the decorum one should have as a Judge, as well as an Attorney, in addition to the teachings of her father, John H. Auld, II, Esq., as a principal of the law firm, Abernethy Auld & Young who has since retired in 2020.

Rebecca is licensed to practice in Pennsylvania and the United States District of the Eastern District of Pennsylvania. With her prior experiences, she brings the same mentality and mindset as counsel while focusing on the client's needs. She competently and passionately assists generations of families.

This life-long resident of Adams Township of Pennsylvania resides with her husband and their three children, who may become the 5th and 6th generations of

Auld Attorneys in Pittsburgh and Texas. When she finds a minute or thirty to spare, Rebecca likes traveling, reading, and cooking for her brood, as well as family and friends.

WEBSITES:
www.AuldBrothersLaw.com

PHONE:
(412) 487-8668 or (412) 487-8666

EMAIL:
RAuld@AuldBrothersLaw.com

INSTAGRAM:
auld_brothers_law_group

NANCY HERMANSEN

CONVERSATION WITH NANCY HERMANSEN

Nancy, you are an attorney with Hermansen Law, based out of Newport Beach, California. Tell us about your practice and the people you help.

Nancy Hermansen: In our elder law practice, I help people avoid the devastating costs of long-term care and empower them to live the quality of life of their choice. Elder law encompasses many fields of law. My firm focuses on helping the senior population plan to preserve their quality of life and protect their income during their lifetime and make a plan for what happens when they pass. As long-term care costs continue to increase, it's important for families to plan ahead and consult with experts familiar with the best strategies based on each family's goals. In our estate planning practice, I help people protect their kids and pass on their stuff without drama and the courts. I work with financial planners, accountants, insurance, and health professionals and take a more holistic approach to legal planning.

> ***What is elder law planning, and how does it differ from traditional estate planning?***

Nancy Hermansen: In elder law planning, we help you as you age to preserve and protect your income and assets for use while you are alive and in need of long-term care. We also help people qualify for government assistance, including Medi-Cal, Veteran's benefits, or healthcare needs. Elder law focuses on the quality of life you want and how to achieve those goals. In traditional estate planning, we are more concerned with what happens after you die and how to distribute what you have to those you love in the way you want while avoiding taxes and conflict.

> ***When is the right time to start planning? Since aging is a sensitive subject, do you find that many people put off planning?***

Nancy Hermansen: Yes, procrastination is the number one reason people put off planning. And I get it; talking about one's death isn't easy and often brings up challenging family dynamics. However, I always say, "The earlier, the better." It's often the adult children in that sandwich generation who become the target point of starting conversations. We start talking with the kids of aging parents to get the parents motivated to come in. Our goal is to intervene and get a plan in place while the senior adult is still competent and can make their own decisions. It's much better to get a plan in place before a loved one has developed any signs of decreased capacity or any kind of dementia or Alzheimer's diagnosis.

What are some common myths and misconceptions surrounding elder law?

Nancy Hermansen: It's a very complex topic, as well as state-specific. It's not a "do it yourself" type of environment. You want to work with professionals familiar with the best strategy, especially because many strategies can be used in places like California. One common myth in elder law is that you have to spend everything you own before you qualify for Medi-Cal long-term care, and that isn't true. We can use trusts or other legal strategies for your unique situation to keep your assets with your family. Also, suppose a loved one can no longer make their own decisions, and no power of attorney or health care agent has been put in place. In that case, the family has to go to court, and those decisions have to be made by a judge who is essentially a stranger to the family. Your loved one may not have their wishes heard or granted when an independent judge just listens to whoever shows up and wants to take part in a public courtroom process.

Another common myth is hiring a lawyer is too expensive for elder law and estate planning issues. Many people think they can handle it on their own in the era of "do-it-yourself" and online forms and services. But just because you can, doesn't mean you should. I recently had a client who used an online platform and thought he had peace of mind. However, upon review of his "done-by-himself" plan, I showed him where his lack of knowledge was going to leave his kids with a minimum $100,000 capital gain tax, and he realized that his "cheap" plan was going to cost a lot more in money, time and frustration.

How do you recommend starting this conversation in families?

Nancy Hermansen: It is all about empowering and allowing your loved one to maintain control. There is a common misconception that getting a lawyer involved or starting to plan takes away control. But it's the opposite of that. The individual gets to make choices and select who will stand in for them if they cannot make decisions one day. While they still have the ability to make choices, they get to plan for the rest of their life and their death. Elder law is really more about life planning than death planning. People feel relieved once they start the process and realize that they're not giving up control. It's more about the adult child beginning the conversation by saying, "I want to help you maintain control and make your own choices. I want to help you live your golden years to the best of your ability and decide how you want to be remembered and how you want the money spent." When making it a positive conversation, most families end up feeling closer than ever.

> *What happens if you are an only child? Do you automatically get power of attorney?*

Nancy Hermansen: There's nothing automatic about these powers. If you don't have a plan in place, it has to go through the court. You have many choices when it comes to your power of attorney. It can be a family member, a close friend, or a corporate fiduciary. It's empowering to know you have options, but making no choice means the court has to decide.

What inspired you to get started in elder law?

Nancy Hermansen: I started my practice within the last year. I was a career prosecutor in the DA's office for 25 years, and I have a passion for helping people in my community and making a difference. I lost both of my parents between 2017 and 2020. Even though I was an attorney, there was a lot I didn't know and learned through the process. Each had a plan in place, which I was grateful for, but I wasn't aware there were more things we could have done to preserve more of their assets that they had worked so hard for. So I decided to make a difference in this area. From my years of experience personally going through it with my parents, I have so much knowledge to share. It's a really underserved area. As our population continues to age, we need people who are passionate about this. I have a more holistic practice, so I have many resources that I can refer my clients to as well.

Is there anything else you would like to share?

Nancy Hermansen: Long-term care costs are skyrocketing, and most people will run out of money in the first year of nursing home care. In California, the average cost is $10,000 per month. And if you need a private caregiver as my parents did, the cost is doubled. Start the process by starting the conversation. It's never too early to plan. You will gain so much peace of mind and can let go of the fear. An elder care lawyer will empower you, not make your situation worse, help preserve your hard-earned assets, and keep your loved ones out of court and conflict.

NANCY HERMANSEN

Attorney, Hermansen Law

Nancy has dedicated her 25+ years as an attorney advocating for and protecting children and families and giving a voice to victims. Nancy spent nearly 25 years as a Deputy District Attorney in both Los Angeles and Orange County and saw firsthand the challenges families face in the legal system. Nancy founded Hermansen Law to empower families to protect their most treasured assets – their children and wealth.

Nancy is a wife and mom of a ten-year-old son and can relate to the family with young children and the fear of what would happen if she and her husband couldn't care for their son. Nancy is personally familiar with all sides of the estate planning and elder law process since she has walked through the death of both of her parents. She knows the elderly population's personal struggles as she helped her mom deal with cancer and a stroke that left her blind and with the onset of Alzheimer's. She helped both of her parents navigate long-term care challenges and expenses, as well as the difficult decision to employ hospice for end-of-life comfort.

Her parents taught her the importance of having an estate plan, and her practice is dedicated to them and her son.

WEBSITE:
https://hermansenlaw.com/

PHONE:
(949)763-3633

EMAIL:

nancy@hermansenlaw.com

FACEBOOK:

https://www.facebook.com/Hermansenlaw

LINKEDIN:

https://www.linkedin.com/in/nancy-hermansen-a8184295/

MATTHEW YAO

Matthew Yao

CONVERSATION WITH MATTHEW YAO

> *Matthew, you are an attorney and partner at Woehrle Dahlberg Yao PLLC, serving all of Virginia. Tell us about your practice and the people you help.*

Matthew Yao: I do a wide range of estate planning which includes drafting estate planning documents, wills, powers of attorney, and trusts. On the other side, which is elder law, I help with guardianships and conservatorships for people who can no longer manage their affairs. This also includes probate for when someone passes away and needs management of assets and trust administration.

> *What concerns do your clients have when they first reach out to you?*

Matthew Yao: The pandemic has caused everyone to have fears about their own mortality. I am getting many calls about estate planning, as people started to realize anything could happen at any time. Younger people tend to want to put off estate planning. Still, the pandemic nudged them to get things in order to ensure that assets go to their children or other designated family members in a straightforward fashion. Wills used to be enough. But wills are not the best way to get your assets assigned to the right people. With a will, there is a process called probate that you have to go through in court. It's a lot of hassle, paperwork, and time. Not to mention, it can be expensive. These days, people are opting for revocable living trusts, which avoids that whole process.

> *What is the danger of not being prepared in the event of your death?*

Matthew Yao: Your family will be left with a big mess. Without a will, everything will have to go through the courts. They will decide who gets your property, and it may not be who you wanted it to go to, depending on your relationships with certain family members. It can be very costly and time-consuming. There is also a bond involved when you pass away without a will. Whoever you want to handle your estate may not be able to do so if they can't qualify for that bond. Various challenges can be easily avoided through proper preparation.

When is the right time to start planning?

Matthew Yao: It's never too soon. I advise people to get started right away. Many people tend to wait until they have children. That's when I see people begin to care about it more. But you should really have something in place even before that. You can always change it later.

What are some common myths and misconceptions surrounding elder law?

Matthew Yao: People think, "Oh, I don't need an estate plan. Nothing is going to happen to me." But if it does, you are going to run into legal problems. What happens if you are still alive but are incapacitated? You definitely need a power of attorney to handle your medical and financial decisions, or nobody will be able to help you when you are unable to decide for yourself.

What inspired you to get started in elder law and estate planning?

Matthew Yao: I just kind of got into it. I did a lot of work with the courts as a guardian *ad litem*, which means I was appointed to help people with guardianship or conservatorship, explain the process, and make sure their rights were protected. So I started there right out of law school. It was a natural progression to elder law and estate planning.

How can people find you, connect with you, and learn more?

Matthew Yao: Our website is www.lawfirmvirginia. com. Feel free to give me a call directly at 703-828-5299 or email me at myao@lawfirmvirginia.com. I would be happy to talk with you.

MATTHEW YAO

Attorney and Partner
Woehrle Dahlberg Yao PLLC

Matthew J. Yao, Esq. is an attorney and owner of Woehrle Dahlberg Yao, PLLC, which has offices throughout Virginia and the DC Metropolitan Area. His practice is focused primarily on Estate Planning and Probate matters. Mr. Yao is an attorney that likes numbers, which is an unusual combination that has made him a highly sought-after administrator of Trusts, Estates, and Conservatorships.

Dedicated to providing excellent service to his clients, Mr. Yao has received recognition and awards from SuperLawyers, BestLawyers, and Virginia Business LegalElite, among others. His clients appreciate his responsiveness and his talent for explaining difficult concepts in simple terms.

Mr. Yao is proud to be a double Hoo, graduating from the University of Virginia's McIntire School of Commerce in 2007 and the UVA School of Law in 2010. He resides in Fairfax, Virginia, with his wife Ellen and their son Moses, where they are very involved with their local church.

WEBSITE:
www.lawfirmvirginia.com

PHONE:
703-828-5299

EMAIL:
myao@lawfirmvirginia.com

MELISSA R. VICTOR

Melissa R. Victor

CONVERSATION WITH MELISSA R. VICTOR

Melissa, you are an elder law and estate planning attorney and owner of Victor & Associates, a law firm based in Southeast Massachusetts. Tell us about your practice and the people you help.

Melissa R. Victor: My main focus for over 24 years has been estate planning and elder law. Estate planning involves wills and trusts. These estate planning documents help people preserve assets by avoiding probate and/or minimizing estate taxes when they pass away. In the elder law realm, I help people protect their assets upon entering a nursing home. I also provide emergency planning for people who haven't prepared beforehand or protected their assets previously.

How has the pandemic affected elder law and the clients that seek you out?

Melissa R. Victor: Several of my clients arrive in my office after someone dies unexpectedly. Perhaps it was someone who passed away at a young age, and they hadn't done any planning. COVID, unfortunately, forced younger and older people to start thinking about death. I had many clients recently who lost mom one week and dad the very next week. It has made people realize how quickly things can happen, even to those that are considered healthy. Most people don't want to think about death. And some even believe that as soon as they put a plan into place, they will pass away. Most of my clients have just realized it is time to stop procrastinating and take action.

What problems can arise from not planning ahead?

Melissa R. Victor: If you have young children and haven't done any planning, your untimely death can hinder them from going to college or having their spouse cared for. Younger generations tend to think they are invincible and nothing will happen to them. But that mindset will ultimately hurt children and spouses.

Once you reach the age of 60 or 70, failing to plan can cost your family thousands of dollars, whether you end up in a nursing home or your estate has to go through probate. The most significant way that people can plan for their family is called a "power of attorney." It's a document that says if you're unable to handle your finances, you name someone to do that for you. And to me, that's the most important estate planning document you can have. Because without it, your family can be forced to go into the probate court in whatever state you live in to become your guardian or conservator in order to be able to handle these assets. A lot of times, when we're dealing with clients, we need to act immediately. And we don't really have time for months in the probate court for somebody to be appointed and for the family to argue. Not planning just causes the family more heartache during an already emotionally difficult time.

Out of my clientele, I would say 1% are people in their 40s and younger. The younger generation rarely wants to put money aside to plan for their death. At the very least, you need to have a will and life insurance in place. But people don't necessarily want to spend the extra money to do that. Especially now with many people being out of work, it's the last thing they want to spend money on.

> ### *Is a will enough? Or is that an old-school way of thinking?*

Melissa R. Victor: We see people getting together to "read the will" in movies all the time. But that doesn't happen in real life. I have never gotten a family together to read the will. I consider the will a basic estate plan for people. It's better than nothing. But on the ladder of estate planning, the will is only the first step. If you have a house, you should have some type of trust. And if you have younger kids, you probably want to have a trust because you don't want them to get the asset when they're 18. Even if you specify an agent in a will, you still bring probate court into it. Anytime we can avoid having the courts involved, it is more beneficial for the family.

> ### *What inspired you to get started in elder law and estate planning?*

Melissa R. Victor: When I was in law school, we had to take a class called "Wills, Estates, and Trusts." It was a core requirement for the bar. I remember thinking about how boring it sounded before I ever took it, and then I loved it! I excelled in that area of law school. And I taught at New England Law in Boston as an adjunct professor for several years when my kids were younger. So I just really enjoyed it. Helping people was a great aspect of it. But it was also an ideal area of law to have a family with because I didn't need to be in court doing criminal trials. I could make my own hours, whether it was day or night. And let's face it, everybody loves kids. So if my child was sick, nobody got angry at me for missing a court date. It was just a really good field for me.

> **If someone is ready to start the planning process, what is the first step they should take?**

Melissa R. Victor: When you're doing estate planning, just like with everything else, you should have somebody specializing in that area. You wouldn't go to a knee doctor to have someone diagnose a problem with your eyes. And it's really the same thing with estate planning. You want to get somebody who knows the different laws regarding probate estate taxes in your particular state. The internet is a great place to start by Googling estate planning attorneys in your area. There are different membership association websites that you can go to, such as the "National Academy of Elder Law Attorneys."

How can people find you and connect with you?

Melissa R. Victor: You can call my office at 508-230-5777. My website is www.attorneyforelders.com. You can find some great information there. I offer a free information session to sit down, understand your plan, and give recommendations. After that, it is in your hands to proceed with whatever you are comfortable doing.

WEBSITE:

www.attorneyforelders.com

PHONE:

508-230-5777

AMANDA L. SMITH

CONVERSATION WITH
AMANDA L. SMITH

> *Amanda, you are an attorney and founder of both the Law Office of Amanda L. Smith, PLLC and Chesapeake Estate Planning Law Firm, a virtual law firm serving Maryland. Tell us about your practice and the people you help.*

Amanda L. Smith: Although I have had my own law firm for over ten years, I am excited to have recently launched a related, yet completely virtual, law practice that focuses on estate planning, elder law, and asset protection. I've taken the hassle out of visiting a brick-and-mortar law office. Nobody wants to talk about estate planning, much less visit their estate planning attorney. So we've taken that out of the mix. I meet with clients all across the state of Maryland through virtual web conferences. I serve a wide range of clients. Some are young families making sure they have guardians in place for their minor children if something happens to the parents. Others are busy professionals in the sandwich generation, trying to protect their businesses, raise families of their own, and provide for their aging parents all at the same time. Finally, I help seniors with estate planning, asset protection, and long-term care planning so they can protect their hard-earned assets and still leave a legacy for their families.

What are common concerns that clients have when they seek you out?

Amanda L. Smith: Especially with the health crisis surrounding the pandemic, I'm seeing many people concerned about being incapacitated, needing healthcare services, and how they would afford that. There is a common misconception that you have to give everything away to afford long-term care. People think they have to lose their house and other assets to qualify for public benefits such as Medicaid. But there are ways that we can protect those assets for clients and their loved ones and still allow them to have quality long-term care services.

> ## What things have to be considered when it comes to long-term care?

Amanda L. Smith: We always look at your income, assets, and goals for what type of facility you want to be in. Do you want to receive care in your own home? Do you want to be in a nursing home or assisted living center with robust care? What care level do you need? Can you qualify for long-term care insurance? Most people want to stay home as long as possible, which can cost a hefty penny. But from a Medicaid qualification standpoint, I look at income, assets, and whether you are married or single. From there, I do an individual analysis and counsel my clients on the various planning strategies to protect their assets while affording long-term care. Some of those strategies may include using asset protection trusts. Sometimes people are fearful when they hear the word "trust" because they think they'll have to give up control of whatever they put in that trust.

With the type of asset protection trust I recommend, clients can maintain control, and they can even be their own trustee calling all the shots just like they did before any assets went into the trust. Do you need to fix the roof of the house? Go for it. Do you want to pay for little Johnny to go to college? Sure thing. Did little Johnny do something wrong, and now you want to take away his inheritance? Done. Maybe he's apologized and made everything right again, and you want to add him back in and even kick in a little extra for all the hardships he faced. Absolutely! Do you want to reinvest your financial portfolio in the latest, greatest stocks? You can. Are you ready to downsize and move into a condo in Florida? Guess what? You can do that, too! You can maintain all of this control while still protecting your assets from long-term care costs. Of course, there are strategies besides an asset protection trust we might implement depending on your particular situation, including Medicaid annuities, special needs trusts, transfers to certain relatives, and more.

In the world of long-term care planning, knowledge is power. Not knowing your options can get you into real trouble, wasting time paying for care out of pocket when you could have a solid long-term care plan in place and feel confident that you've adequately planned for and protected your family's future.

What are common mistakes people make in long-term care planning?

Amanda L. Smith: I teach nationally on the topic of Medicaid planning, specifically in long-term care

planning. I hear horror stories, not just in my practice but from attorneys all across the country, about
things clients did on their own before coming into a
law office. Perhaps they've given their house away to
their kids, thinking they needed to get rid of it to qualify for Medicaid. In reality, most homes are exempt for
Medicaid purposes. Many people make some sort of hap-
hazard gifts to loved ones, whether their home or other
assets, without realizing they will incur a Medicaid gifting penalty. Now, you're left without any money to pay
your long-term care costs because you gave it all away,
and you have to wait around for that penalty to expire
before Medicaid starts paying for your care. This could
go on for months or even years, placing a huge burden
on your family members. That's the most common mistake; the gifting that people mess up on the front end
before they see an attorney, and we have to find a way to
remedy some of that. When we give away purposefully
to the right people in the right manner, we can protect
assets AND qualify for benefits.

Another mistake people make is waiting too long to put
an estate plan in place. I always tell people it's never
too late to plan, but unfortunately, I've seen too many
instances where people lose many of their available options because they waited too long. For example, not
giving someone the ability to make your health care and
financial decisions before you need it can be costly - in

both time and money. Although we can still clean up the mess, so to speak, it is always better to plan earlier while the most options and strategies are on the table.

You also have to make sure you have a personalized estate plan, not mere documents. You know the kind that you can print off online or that you get from an attorney who only dabbles in estate planning? You wouldn't trust your heart surgery to an eye doctor, right? You wouldn't watch a YouTube video, buy a scalpel, and operate on yourself either. So, don't trust your estate and long-term care planning to just anyone. You want to make sure the person walking you through these crucial decisions knows their stuff and all of the distinct rules of law that apply to your unique circumstances.

> *What is the typical client experience like with your virtual firm?*

Amanda L. Smith: Your estate planning journey begins when you attend one of our virtual estate planning Workshops, which highlights key estate planning concepts and, most importantly, enlightens you to the things you didn't even know to consider as part of your comprehensive estate plan.

After viewing the Workshop, you're ready for a Vision Meeting to review any existing estate planning documents. Based on your key takeaways from the Workshop, we work to solidify your vision for an estate plan that's just right for your individual goals. You will leave with some homework (but not the boring stuff you had back in high school) to prepare for the next step of the process – the Design Meeting.

At the Design Meeting, you'll be counseled through many planning decisions. This is when you decide who gets your stuff, when, where, and how. You'll also be naming the key players in your estate plan – those that will make important decisions on your behalf. Now your vision starts to become a reality.

At your Plan Presentation Meeting, you will preview your documents for clarity and accuracy. I give detailed instructions on properly signing your documents and making any asset transfers or beneficiary designation changes needed to accomplish your vision.

An estate plan only works if properly signed and assets are allocated correctly based on your goals. That's why we have a crucial Review Meeting after you've signed your documents and made any asset changes required. As part of your estate planning engagement, your attorney will review the signed documents for accuracy and ensure you have the most up-to-date listing of assets for your records. For those clients who elect to participate in our Client Maintenance Program, you have the added benefit of a yearly Virtual Maintenance Review Meeting to ensure your plan evolves as your family's circumstances change over the years.

What inspired you to get started in estate planning and elder law?

Amanda L. Smith: I've been focused on this area of law for 11 years now. It is an area that allows me to take my passion for planning (I'm a planner by nature) and help families in all phases of life. I've got my own grandparents and people close to me who have gone through things like this, and I have the privilege of helping them navigate the challenges of long-term care while still having the very best quality of life. So I get to practice law, but in a less contentious environment than litigation. My clients are typically happy people just looking to make the best out of their current situation. So it's an area of law that I get a lot of satisfaction from because of the relationships I'm able to build with the many families I help each day.

How can people connect with you and learn more?

Amanda L. Smith: My website is www.chesapeakes-tateplanning.com. From the events tab, you'll see that I do several estate planning workshops designed to give people all the information they need to start making informed decisions about their estate plans. You can sign up right from the website. These are complimentary workshops that last for about an hour. You can also call the firm at 888-EPLawFirm, that's 888-375-2934, or email me directly at amanda@chesapeakeestateplanning.com.

AMANDA L. SMITH

Attorney and Founder
Law Office of Amanda L. Smith, PLLC
and
Chesapeake Estate Planning Law Firm

Compassionate problem solver: that is the phrase used by many to describe Amanda. She is always looking to learn new things and help people, devoting much of her life to discovering new ways to help others solve problems or reach their goals. Whether in her personal or professional life, Amanda is the go-to resource for those looking for guidance amid chaos or seemingly insurmountable obstacles.

Amanda has been a national speaker on the topics of estate planning, Medicaid, and asset protection. She is focused on bridging the technology gap in the legal field between attorneys and their clients and recently served as Director of Legal & Technology. She led projects focusing on technical innovation for the estate planning industry.

Amanda founded the Law Office of Amanda L. Smith, PLLC, in 2010 and, more recently, launched a completely virtual estate planning, elder law, and asset protection firm of Chesapeake Estate Planning Law Firm. She mixes her southern charm with a bit of technical know-how, providing clients with a friendly, nurturing, and seamless experience from start to finish, easing the burdens and anxieties usually associated with visiting a traditional law firm.

Education

- University of Arkansas at Little Rock William H. Bowen School of Law, J.D., with honors, 2010
- Arkansas State University, B.S. Finance, cum laude, 2006

Bar Admissions

- Maryland
- Texas

Professional & Community Involvement

- Maryland State Bar Association
- Texas Bar Association
- Former Board of Directors of local HOA
- Volunteer Youth Volleyball Coach
- Former Board Member for Community Youth Athletic Club

Amanda is married to her amazing husband, Nic, and together the couple has three children, Evan, Ryan, and Avenly, and two fur babies, Baxter and Bailey.

LEADING ELDER LAW AND ESTATE PLANNING ATTORNEYS

—— **WEBSITE:** ——
www.chesapeakeestateplanning.com

—— **PHONE:** ——
888-375-2934 888-EPLawFirm

—— **EMAIL:** ——
amanda@chesapeakeestateplanning.com

—— **FACEBOOK:** ——
https://www.facebook.com/Chesapeake-Estate-Planning-La
w-Firm-114260710432699

—— **LINKEDIN:** ——
https://www.linkedin.com/in/amanda-l-smith-esq-a1475391/

SAMANTHA MCCARTHY

Samantha Mccarthy

CONVERSATION WITH ATTORNEY SAMANTHA MCCARTHY

Samantha, you are an elder law and estate planning attorney serving Rhode Island and Massachusetts. Tell us about your practice and the people you help.

Samantha McCarthy: In the Estate Planning side of my practice, I serve people all the way from college age through retirement and beyond. We work with individuals and families, both young and old, to create customized, thorough estate plans to help secure their future and provide peace of mind that both the client and their family are provided for and protected in the future, for both the anticipated and the unknown. These plans include financial and healthcare powers of attorney, living wills, last will and testaments, and trusts.

The Elder law side of my practice is really a subset specialty in the estate planning world. Elder law focuses on the aging population and ensures that older individuals have the care they need and the money to pay for that care. A big part of my elder law practice is helping people who can't safely live alone at home anymore. When this time comes, several issues arise, including what the right level of care is going forward and how the client and their family can afford to pay for that care. Clients in this situation often come to us with their families asking questions such as, "Is assisted living an option? How do we get into a nursing home? How much will this all cost? Will I lose everything? Are there any government benefits available to help pay for this care?"

We help clients evaluate options such as private duty in-home care, assisted living, nursing home care, and at times hospice to formulate a customized care plan that is best suited to the individual client and their needs. And throughout all these decisions, we evaluate both the level of care needed in conjunction with the cost of that care, the client's resources that are available to pay for that care, or the government benefits available to assist with payment.

Additionally, we evaluate different planning techniques available to potentially save a client's hard-earned money and assets so that they don't lose everything they have worked for their entire life because they suddenly need a higher level of care than can be supported at home. Many seniors are afraid to ask for help as they age because they are afraid of the cost of such help and afraid they will lose everything. That is frequently not the case, and often the hardest part is reaching out to ask for help. But once you have the right professional on your side, they will help walk you through and navigate the process in the best way possible. We are successfully able to help many clients with long-term care and Medicaid planning. People work really hard their whole lives for their money, and then they fear losing their assets to a nursing home. We help people plan to ensure that doesn't happen.

> **What are some common challenges your clients face?**

Samantha McCarthy: In the Elder Law section of my practice, people often don't realize there are options at the last minute. Many of my clients hear about a "five-year look-back rule," where the government will see if you transferred any assets for less than fair market value or made any gifts during that time. And if they haven't planned ahead five years or more, many people think they are out of options. In reality, there are still several options, even at the last minute and even when someone has already entered a nursing home. But everybody hears from their neighbor or their friend or their cousin that so and so lost their house when they entered a nursing home, so people are afraid to reach out for help before they even get started. It is important to keep in mind that everyone's situation is different, and how the law applies to the specific facts of your situation may be different. The available planning techniques may be different. Important questions to consider include: Are you married? Do you own real estate? What other property do you have? What accounts do you have? How are your assets titled? What funds do you have invested? Are those funds held in qualified (tax-deferred) or non-qualified accounts? People will often come to me and say, "My neighbor lost their house, and I don't want that to happen to me." But that may not even be possible based on their own circumstances, so the most important thing to know is that there are options available, and just don't wait too long to reach out for help. You don't know what you don't know, but if you have the right professional to support you through the process, the situation often is not as daunting as it may seem.

Similarly, in the estate planning part of my practice, misconceptions regarding available planning techniques like wills versus trusts, and when a family should or should not have certain estate planning documents in place often lead individuals and families to wait longer than they should to create a plan. At a basic level, anyone who is a legal adult should have basic powers of attorney in place. And if you have young children, guardianship designations and asset protection planning are super important. As a single mom of two young children, I know firsthand how important it is to designate who would take care of my babies if something happened to me and provide structure around how life insurance proceeds and other assets would be managed for their benefit.

What are some misconceptions in your field of law?

Samantha McCarthy: The biggest misconceptions in the Elder Law part of my practice include what assets are considered available to pay for long-term care and which are not. For instance, in Rhode Island, retirement accounts are not considered an available resource to pay for your care, but in many other states, they are. Additionally, contrary to what many people believe, the state (or the nursing home) won't ever take someone's house while they are living; however, they may file a lien against that home after the person's death to recover what the state paid out for that person's care. So people think everything will go to the nursing home, and that's just not the case. If you have a community spouse, there are certain assets you're allowed to keep. And if you don't have a community spouse, you might not be allowed to keep those same assets. There is a lot of fear-based discussion amongst seniors, which is understandable. But we try to cut through that and help people see how they can get the care they need without losing everything.

On the estate planning side, the biggest misconception is that a will is a thorough estate plan and avoids probate upon death. In reality, all a will does is guarantee probate. A will tells the probate court what you want to happen to your things and who you want to manage the process of collecting and distributing assets, but all of that still has to happen under the overview of the court. People also think if they have a will, everything they own will pass subject to the provisions of their will. However, the only assets that pass subject to a person's will are assets they own in their name alone, without a designated beneficiary. So, it follows then that to avoid probate; you must not own assets in your name alone without a designated beneficiary. And that is where trust planning comes in so that people don't have to give away assets immediately but can provide a plan for their assets to avoid probate and provide for their loved ones.

How early should people start planning?

Samantha McCarthy: The earlier, the better. If we're talking about long-term care planning and elder law, five years is the key time frame right now. It might be seven years in the future. When you don't have a significant health crisis, that's a good time to be making the plan so that when you do, you have had the plan in place far enough in advance to save everything you have.

When it comes to estate planning, anyone over the age of 18 should have powers of attorney. College students should have powers of attorney that allow their parents to manage their finances and pay their bills, access their medical information, and talk to doctors if something happens to them.

My clients stretch from college-age young adults to parents with young children, through about-to-retire and recently retired people moving on to the next phase of their lives, all the way through seniors. Then we also help families through the dying process and then probate after death when necessary.

COVID has really brought awareness to the fact that we are all going to die at some point. Due to this, over the last year or so, we have seen younger and younger clients coming in. Nobody wants to talk about dying, and many people avoid the estate planning process for entirely too long because of it. But, I always say to my clients, "If you make the plan now, then you can put it away. You can forget about it for a while, but you can also sleep well at night knowing you have a plan to protect what you worked so hard for and the people you love."

And estate planning really is not just about dying. It is also about asset protection during a person's life, as well as planning for accidents and incapacity, so that we maintain the right to decide who would make decisions for us in both the financial and medical arenas in the event we are not able to speak for ourselves, whether temporarily or long term. Without a proper estate plan, if an accident or emergency happens, it can be left up to a court to decide who will make financial and healthcare decisions for a person. So people should plan ahead and have the autonomy to make those decisions for themselves.

Can you tell us about trusts and how they protect people?

Samantha McCarthy: There are several different kinds of trusts. At the most basic level is a revocable trust where you maintain control of your own assets. So anything you're able to do now, you can do through a revocable trust. If properly funded, this kind of trust avoids probate court upon death and provides for management and distribution of assets for loved ones or charities. As I mentioned before, a prevalent misconception is that you are all set if you have a will. But the only thing a will guarantees is that you are going to probate. The will tells the world what you want to happen and who you want to manage the process of transferring your things, but it requires probate court oversight. So a trust, if properly funded, allows you to avoid that. I like to think of a will and a trust both as expensive pieces of paper that say what you want to happen to your stuff when you pass away. But the trust has a bucket attached to it that can hold assets, so we look to the trust for the rules about what happens with the things in that bucket after your death, rather than looking to the court with a will. The trust also provides additional asset protection mechanisms for beneficiaries. For instance, perhaps you don't want all of your assets going to your children if they are still very young, or maybe you have a beneficiary with special needs or financial problems. The trust will lay out exactly how you want assets to be managed and by whom so that they benefit your loved ones in the way you feel most comfortable with.

There are also more complex trusts, such as irrevocable trusts, which can provide asset protection in the event nursing home care is needed in the future and tax planning.

What inspired you to get started in elder law and estate planning?

Samantha McCarthy: I grew up living next door to my grandfather, who had Multiple Sclerosis. On a day-to-day basis, I saw the difficulty my family had accessing services and finding the right information needed to provide for him. If you're really wealthy, you can afford to pay someone for 24-7 care in your home. If you're poor, you can get Medicaid to help. But if you are somewhere in the middle, you're not poor enough for the government to help you, but not wealthy enough to pay out of pocket for services. This creates a significant access to service issue. I saw everything we had to do as a family to make sure my grandfather was protected and provided for and my grandmother so that she would not lose everything if something happened to him. So all of that inspired me to say, "There's a need here." There is a need for people to be cared for in a compassionate way, which sometimes gets lost in the law and with lawyers.

I can bring understanding to my clients on a very personal level and a professional one.

Additionally, on the estate planning side, I grew up with divorced parents and now have gone through a divorce myself, so I am a single mom of two young children. Together with my partner, we have three kids in our blended family. As a result, I understand the complexity of planning for various family dynamics that are very common in today's families and society. As I like to say, "every family has their stuff," and no two families are exactly alike, which is why estate planning needs to be a customized process to meet clients' individual needs.

Is there anything else you would like to share?

Samantha McCarthy: The most important thing to remember is that you don't have to have all the answers. If you're working with the right professional, they will ask you the right questions and help organize the information and process to make it less complex. Many people are afraid to start the process because they don't have everything together. But the most important part is making the call and scheduling a consultation with a knowledgeable and experienced professional. Then the attorney can walk you through the process. Talking about dying is not as scary when you actually do it and have someone to support you through the process. Just get your asset list together and make the call.

> ### *How can people connect with you and learn more?*

Samantha McCarthy: You can find us online at www.mccarthylawri.com, reach the office via email at MLoffice@ mccarthylawri.com, or via telephone at 401-541-5540.

SAMANTHA MCCARTHY, ESQ.

Attorney-at-Law
McCarthy Law, LLC

Samantha McCarthy is an Estate Planning and Elder Law attorney in Rhode Island and Massachusetts. She is a member of the Rhode Island Bar Association, the Rhode Island Bar Association's Probate and Trust Committee, the National Academy of Elder Law Attorneys (NAELA), the Rhode Island chapter of NAELA, and the Board of Directors at the Hope Alzheimer's Center in Cranston, Rhode Island where she also serves as Secretary of the Board. Samantha earned her Juris Doctor degree from Roger Williams University School of Law and her undergraduate degree at North Dakota State University. She was named a Rhode Island Super Lawyers Rising Star in 2019, 2020, and 2021. In addition, she was chosen by Rhode Island Monthly for the 2021 Professional Excellence in Law award for Elder Law.

Her passion for Estate Planning and Elder Law began long before she became a lawyer. From seeing her grandfather's struggles, living with Multiple Sclerosis for many years, she was inspired to become involved with disability activism work during college. Through that work and her own family experience, she saw the real impact proper planning could have for families and what a difference it could make both during life and after one's passing.

Samantha founded McCarthy Law to make a meaningful impact in the lives of others. She prides herself on being approachable and compassionate and believes in developing relationships with her clients that allow both parties to grow and learn. She believes her clients are amazing people who teach her new things about life and the world every day, and she is so grateful for the opportunity to serve them and be there for her clients as a partner through life's best and most challenging times.

WEBSITE:
www.mccarthylawri.com

PHONE:
401-541-5540

EMAIL:
MLoffice@mccarthylawri.com

FACEBOOK:
https://www.facebook.com/mccarthylawllc

INSTAGRAM:
https://www.instagram.com/mccarthylawllc/

LINKEDIN:
https://www.linkedin.com/company/mccarthylawllc

WENDY MARA

Wendy Mara

CONVERSATION WITH WENDY MARA

Wendy, you are an attorney and the founder of Mara Law. Tell us about your practice and the people you help.

Wendy Mara: We do estate planning, which really isn't just elder law. It goes right across the spectrum from 18 years old until somebody passes away. But we find that most of our clients are over the age of 50, maybe even over 55. When you're younger, you tend to think nothing will happen, and you don't have to worry about estate planning. But as people become older, and especially with COVID, our practice has been extremely busy. People are worried now more than ever. Is something going to happen to me? Will I be living but unable to make medical and financial decisions on my own? Am I going to pass away?

Part of estate planning is Medicaid planning. People sometimes think about food stamps and similar assistance when they hear the term "Medicaid," but we focus on the long-term care planning aspect of Medicaid when someone needs to enter a skilled nursing facility. In Florida, that's the most common assistance we provide. We also have waiver programs for people who want supplemental help for in-home care and care in an assisted living facility. However, there is a waitlist for waiver programs. Skilled nursing facilities do not involve waitlists.

We also handle guardianships. The most common type of guardianship in elder law is when somebody who has developed Alzheimer's or dementia can no longer take care of themselves. So, somebody steps in and files for guardianship. And there is also a voluntary guardianship for somebody who feels that they can no longer take care of their financial matters. However, the potential ward needs to have capacity and agree to have a guardianship for a voluntary guardianship. This guardianship handles property and takes care of financial matters. We've also begun doing some veterans administration benefits because we continue to see areas to better service our clients.

> ## *What concerns do clients have when they first reach out to you?*

Wendy Mara: Unfortunately, many people reach out to us when they have a loved one who has not planned properly. They ask if we can have the person sign power of attorney and health care surrogate, but they are already incapacitated. We can't do that. When someone is signing documents, they must understand what they are signing. So in a situation like that, if there are no estate planning documents prepared and signed, then you're forced into a guardianship. I always tell my clients that guardianship is the last resort. You do not want to have to do that. And so you can do the simple estate plan with a will, a power of attorney, and a healthcare surrogate. You can also choose a guardian in advance. It is only a few hundred dollars to do all of that. On the other hand, a guardianship will cost thousands of dollars, and the courts are involved until the ward passes away or capacity is restored, which is rare. If you have a situation with somebody with Alzheimer's or dementia, it's not going to go away. It's actually going to get worse. So it's very expensive at that point. My recommendation to everybody is you need to get at least the basic estate planning done. It's sad when I have clients come in and talk to me, and they don't have the money to do the guardianship. They would have been able to handle the cost of the estate planning if they had gone that route first. So it ends up being a very tough situation.

> ### *What are some of the consequences of not being adequately prepared?*

Wendy Mara: If you don't have a healthcare surrogate in place, then there's nobody who can make healthcare decisions on your behalf. If there is no power of attorney appointed, there's nobody who can make financial decisions on your behalf. And doctors are getting more and more strict with the information they give out to family members because of HIPAA laws. If someone tries to handle paying your bills or your mortgage, the mortgage company will not talk to that person without power of attorney. Companies are very strict about giving out confidential information. So then you end up with a situation where somebody's house could go into foreclosure because nobody knows how to go about paying the mortgage. Some people have things on automatic payment, and that might work for a while. But eventually, you're going to run into a situation where something needs to be done that nobody has the legal ability to handle.

What happens if nobody is appointed as a guardian?

Wendy Mara: Well, somebody has to file for guardianship. Sometimes, if someone is being neglected or if there is a serious situation, DCFS will come in and make some recommendations. They have the authority to do that. A nonprofit organization is appointed to handle guardianships for public guardians for people who don't have money in each judicial circuit. But there's a backup of that. Here in our area, the Council on Aging handles public guardians. I happen to be the Chair of the Elder Law Section of the Volusia County Bar. And they reached out to the Volusia County Bar, asking for volunteers and pro bono attorneys to handle some of the backlogs of public guardian cases. A guardian must have an attorney in the state of Florida unless it's a parent who's filing on behalf of a developmentally disabled adult.

> *If someone is incapacitated and hasn't*
> *properly made these appointments, can an*
> *adult child or another family member apply*
> *for guardianship?*

Wendy Mara: Yes. Sometimes the family member who is applying will ask to be appointed as guardian. Other times, the person who is applying asks for a professional guardian to be appointed. In other cases, we recommend that the Council on Aging be appointed because they also handle private guardianships. So if family members don't feel up to serving as guardians, there are professionals that can handle it for you. The ones that I have had interactions with are excellent and very compassionate. They don't just see it as a job. This is really a calling because it's a 24-7 responsibility.

> *What is the first step to making a plan for your*
> *family?*

Wendy Mara: Look for an attorney to help you navigate the type of estate planning you need for your unique situation. It's not a one-size-fits-all. What are your assets? Do you have minor children? Do you have children or beneficiaries with special needs? Do you have a beneficiary with addiction or gambling problems? You wouldn't want to leave money to those individuals. So it really depends on your family situation. Reach out and speak to an attorney. I've had to do probates on cases where people decided to do their own wills, and nine times out of ten, it is a complete disaster. The outcome is not what they had hoped. And then the family is upset. But by law, you have to go with what a will says, and sometimes wills are drafted and then not executed properly. So they're not valid. We've had deeds that were not valid. Relatively speaking, simple estate planning is not expensive. When you're talking about transferring a home and other accounts, spending a few hundred dollars to make sure those large assets are appropriately transferred is well worth the cost of working with an attorney.

> *Should people be looking for an estate planning attorney, an elder law attorney, or a combination of both?*

Wendy Mara: If you are looking specifically to have a will package drafted, you can call your local bar to find an estate planning attorney. The Florida Bar has a list of attorneys and different practice areas. So you can reach out to the Florida Bar and get a list of attorneys. You can also ask around. Financial planners and CPAs are great people to ask. You certainly want to find an attorney you trust and feel comfortable with since they will be helping you to make major life decisions. It doesn't hurt to speak with a few attorneys until you find a good match.

> ## What inspired you to get into elder law and estate planning?

Wendy Mara: Well, I live in Florida. Most people know there are quite a few elderly people here in Florida. I got an MBA before I went to law school, and I planned to do business law. I actually did that for a year, and I didn't find it to be terribly exciting. It just so happened I was working with Community Legal Services of Florida, which is a nonprofit agency. As a legal aid, I asked them what they needed help with, and they said guardianships. So I started doing it pro bono. I felt like I was really helping people, and it felt good. So I decided to start offering these services to my paying clients. It expanded into estate planning and Medicaid long-term care planning because I recognized some of my clients needed help in those areas. And then, of course, the next step was to get into the VA planning because those sometimes interact. You don't want to do one thing to help with Medicaid and then end up hurting the VA realm. So I like to make sure I am giving my clients good advice.

> ***How can people connect with you and learn more?***

Wendy Mara: I'm in Ormond Beach, which is Volusia County. We are directly north of Daytona Beach. As far as litigation, we stick to Volusia and Flagler counties. We handle probates all over the state. Most people will want to be pretty close for estate planning since they come into the office to sign documents. We provide Zoom and phone consultations, but all documents must be signed in person. As things are opening up, we can go to hospitals and nursing homes for people who aren't mobile and can't come to us.

Our phone number is 386-672-8081. You can find us on the web at www.maralawpa.com. We would love to hear from any of your readers.

WENDY MARA

Attorney and Founder
Mara Law, P.A.

Wendy A. Mara is the managing attorney at Mara Law, P.A. ("Mara Law") with Ormond Beach and Palm Coast offices. Mara Law focuses on protecting individuals, their families, and their assets in the areas of Family Law, Probate, Guardianship, Estate, and Medicaid Planning.

Ms. Mara earned a BA from Stetson University, her MBA from the University of Central Florida, and her J.D. from Florida Coastal School of Law. She has consistently received top-ranked reviews on Martindale Hubbell, Lawyers.com, Findlaw, AVVO, Linked-In, and Facebook.

Ms. Mara is currently Chair of the Eastern Deanery of the Catholic Foundation of Central Florida Planned Giving Advisory Board, Chair of the Elder Law Section of the Volusia County Bar Association (VCBA), and a Den Leader for Cub Scout Pack 74. She is a former member of the Board of Directors of the Ormond Beach Chamber of Commerce ("OBCC"), past chair of PACE Center for Girls, Volusia-Flagler, past President of the Volusia Flagler Association for Women Lawyers ("VFAWL"), and past President of the VCBA. Ms. Mara provides legal assistance to indigent clients on behalf of Community Legal Services of Mid Florida (CLSMF) and Council on Aging. She serves as a Guardian ad Litem for children in Flagler and Volusia Counties.

Ms. Mara received the Leadership Award in 2013 from OBCC. In addition, Ms. Mara was named the VFAWL "Woman of the Year" in 2015 for her work on behalf of women and girls. Ms. Mara is AV-rated by Martindale Hubbell and named a Rising Star Super Lawyer in 2016-2019, an honor held by less than 2.5% of Florida attorneys. In addition, Ms. Mara has been recognized multiple times by CLSMF for her pro bono work.

Ms. Mara has six children, three grandchildren, and resides in Ormond Beach with her husband, Robert.

WEBSITE:

www.maralawpa.com

PHONE:

386-672-8081

SHERI L. MONTECALVO

Sheri L. Montecalvo

CONVERSATION WITH SHERI L. MONTECALVO

> *Sheri, you are an attorney and the founder of Estate Planning With Sheri, serving Rhode Island, Massachusetts, and Connecticut. Tell us about your practice and the people you help.*

Sheri L. Montecalvo: I am an elder law and estate planning attorney. We focus on estate planning, long-term care planning, disability planning, and probate and trust administration. Our clients range from young to old, and the majority are middle-aged or around 65, looking for estate planning and asset protection.

What concerns do your clients have when they seek you out?

Sheri L. Montecalvo: The pandemic really changed things. Many of my clients realize that you can be young and healthy yet still face something with a chance of mortality. And with that, you need to have your estate planning documents in order. One of the major misconceptions is that people think they're too young to worry about estate planning.

However, you're never too young to engage in estate planning because, as the pandemic has shown us, you can be confronted with a sudden illness or accident and need documents to protect you in the event of incapacitation or death. The pandemic has had a somewhat positive effect in making people realize the importance of estate planning. On the negative side, courts are running with half of their staff, so probate administration has gone from a slow process to an even SLOWER process. This can be very difficult for families who are already experiencing so many emotional challenges.

What are some of the consequences of not planning properly?

Sheri L. Montecalvo: You're leaving everything up to chance. If you have children, why wouldn't you want to nominate a guardian for them? If you have assets, why wouldn't you want to divide them amongst the people of your choosing? If you fail to plan, plan to fail. Procedures will take much longer, and other beneficiaries or interested parties can assert an interest and have a say in your estate administration. If you formalize your intentions in a will, this document speaks at the time of your death, and your written decision upholds your wishes.

By implementing an estate plan, you can also reduce or eliminate taxes and provide protections for distributions to minors and those beneficiaries facing unusual circumstances (i.e., litigation or substance abuse problems). If you don't have a will, your estate will be an estate administration, and the assets will be divided according to the laws of intestacy of the domicile of the decedent. Your estate could be left to a beneficiary that you didn't want to leave it to. Most importantly, with guardian provisions regarding minors, you could have anyone petitioning the court for guardianship of your minor children. I believe most parents would want the opportunity to choose someone they have confidence in.

Additionally, without an estate plan, a guardian or conservator would be required to be appointed in the event of incapacitation. This can be a timely and costly procedure that most people would prefer to avoid.

Is a will enough? Or do people need more than that?

Sheri L. Montecalvo: One of the top misconceptions about estate planning is that you just need a basic will. Well, in addition to that, you need to prepare for incapacitation. Therefore, I would recommend adding a durable general power of attorney, which is a financial power of attorney, a healthcare power of attorney, and a HIPPA authorization in the event that you became incapacitated. These three things, at a minimum, are your essential documents.

Some clients don't realize other vehicles may be better for them. A revocable inter vivos trust, which comes into existence now during the client's lifetime, will grow with them and their assets. Some clients feel that this is more financially than they want to commit to, but in the end, this plan will save the client valuable time and money on expensive probate fees in the long run. When my clients come to me wanting a basic will, I take them through the entire process and present them with all options to make an educated decision.

When is the right time for people to start planning?

Sheri L. Montecalvo: As soon as you are an adult, you can draft your own will and powers of attorney. It's a common misconception that you have to possess assets. At a minimum, the client should have a will and powers of attorney in place to prepare for incapacitation or passing. Furthermore, once you have a material change such as getting married, having children, getting a divorce, or coming into any type of inheritance, it is important to update your estate plan. I tell my clients to update me on any changes or life advancements and regularly every three to five years.

What inspired you to get started in elder law and estate planning?

Sheri L. Montecalvo: It has always been a passion of mine. I enjoy seeing and serving the family generations. Personally, it's a wonderful experience to know that I assisted mom and dad with their plan, and they had enough confidence in me to recommend me to their children or a family member/friend. I am with my clients as a trusted advisor throughout the generations, and we have a close family relationship. Clients send me thank you cards and wedding pictures. It is gratifying to create estate plans that meet my client's goals and needs.

How can people connect with you and learn more?

Sheri L. Montecalvo: My Facebook page is Estate Planning With Sheri, https://www.facebook.com/Estate-Planning-With-Sheri-100131601394557. I also have a website: www.estateplanningwithsheri.com. Feel free to call me directly at 401-471-6034. LinkedIn: linkedin.com/in/sheri-montecalvo-9507973.

SHERI L. MONTECALVO, ESQ.

Attorney and Founder
Estate Planning With Sheri

Sheri L. Montecalvo, Esq., concentrates her practice in the areas of estate and tax planning, asset protection planning, business succession planning, corporate, elder law, probate, guardianship, trust and estate administration, special needs planning, and Medicaid planning. She has over 15 years of experience providing counsel to business owners, individuals, and families. Sheri takes pride in serving as a trusted advisor to her long-standing clients and their future family generations. She sees her clients through the entire process from document creation, re-titling of assets, and complete estate/trust administration. Sheri is a graduate of Roger Williams School of Law, Juris Doctorate, cum laude, Pupilage Chambers of Michael Parroy, Q.C., London, England, and Rhode Island College, B.A., magna cum laude. Sheri has the following Bar Admissions: State of Rhode Island, Commonwealth of Massachusetts, State of Connecticut, United States District Court for the District of Rhode Island, United States District Court for the District of Massachusetts, United States Supreme Court. Her office is located in Rhode Island, and she resides in Connecticut with her husband, three children, and beloved animals.

WEBSITE:
www.estateplanningwithsheri.com

PHONE:
401-471-6034 or 401-300-1429

EMAIL:
smontecalvo@mymlgpc.com or smontecalvo@outlook.com

FACEBOOK:

Estate Planning With Sheri
https://www.facebook.com/Estate-Planning-With-
Sheri-100131601394557

LINKEDIN:

linkedin.com/in/sheri-montecalvo-9507973

SHARON RUTBERG

Sharon Rutberg

CONVERSATION WITH SHARON RUTBERG

> *Sharon, you are an attorney with Salmon Bay Law Group, based in Seattle, Washington. Tell us about your practice and the people you help.*

Sharon Rutberg: Thank you for the opportunity to provide a general overview of my law practice. Please keep in mind that my responses are not legal advice! Folks with legal questions should contact me or another estate planning or elder law attorney -- more on that later.

Elder law is an umbrella term that covers a variety of legal practice areas. Estate planning involves planning for after you pass away. It includes setting up wills and trusts to direct where your assets go at your death, minimize estate taxation, protect vulnerable beneficiaries, and so on. But we also plan for life, working with clients to get durable powers of attorney and health care directives in place so people they trust can help them as they get older or incapacitated.

We also look at long-term care planning, which is a huge issue right now. This includes applying for benefits to cover the cost of long-term care, whether at home or in a care facility, and seeking to preserve the family's assets. Some elder law attorneys also focus on guardianship or elder abuse. My focus is on estate planning, probate, and helping people plan for long-term care situations.

What are the primary concerns of your current clients?

Sharon Rutberg: We have a long-term care crisis in this country. Many of the baby boomers are now in their 70s. As we age, doctors can keep us alive for a long time, but many people begin to need a lot of help with medical and personal care. In fact, some 70 percent of people are estimated to need some type of long-term care in their lifetime. This could mean getting help from family members, bringing care into the home, moving to an assisted living facility or adult family home, or going to a skilled nursing facility -- the classic nursing home. Many people will need this type of service, and it can be very expensive, especially if you don't have a family equipped to care for you full time.

Many people do not realize that Medicare and health insurance will not pay for long-term care. At most, you might get 100 days of skilled nursing assistance with Medicare, and then you may either be sent home or moved to a facility that costs several thousand dollars a month. That can start to drain a family's resources. Wealthier families may be able to pay privately, and a minority of people have purchased long-term care insurance. The Medicaid program is a set of government benefits that acts as a safety net for everyone else.

There are ways for people to get Medicaid benefits to cover their long-term care expenses while preserving some of their assets. For example, a married couple may be able to move assets over to the "well" spouse, get the sick spouse qualified for benefits, and avoid spending down all of the family's resources. But people don't know what the rules are -- there's a lot of misinformation out there. And the rules are very complicated. So we're eager to help people learn what their options are ahead of time before a crisis happens.

What are the benefits of early planning?

Sharon Rutberg: We love to see people who come in early and say, "Hey, I'm getting older. I might need to move to assisted living at some point. What can I afford, and how should I plan?" Or "My husband is getting sicker and might need a nursing home one of these days. How do we pay for it and keep enough for me to live on?" All of this is easier to tackle when we plan in advance.

Crisis mode gets more complicated. In crisis mode, perhaps mom breaks her hip, and the rehab facility is about to send her home. How will you pay for her care? In that case, we may have a month or two to get mom qualified for benefits and preserve resources. Many people are misinformed and say, "Well, I'm going to have to sell my house." But in our state, depending on your circumstances, you may be able to qualify for Medicaid benefits and still keep your home. Your spouse can continue to live in the house and can have income and resources to live on. If the sick spouse is in a nursing home, Medicaid can help pay the monthly cost, which can be $10,000 to $15,000 per month or more in my area. Even if you're unmarried, there may be ways to get you qualified for Medicaid benefits without spending every dime of your money. Working with a qualified elder law attorney when these situations arise is important.

Do people need more than just a basic will?

Sharon Rutberg: We usually hear from clients, "I want to redo my will." It's great to have a will. Every state has a law that says where your property and assets will go when you die. If you don't have a will, then your assets will pass according to your state's law, and it may not be what you want. A properly drafted will can direct who will get your assets, minimize your exposure to estate taxation, protect assets in a trust for younger or disabled beneficiaries, even provide for a beloved pet. So having a will in place is good -- and it's not usually enough.

We almost always create a whole package of documents for our clients, including durable powers of attorney and advance directives. Durable powers of attorney are one of the most powerful tools you can have to protect your interests while you are alive. A durable power of attorney is a document that authorizes the person of your choice to handle your affairs when you can't do it yourself. Perhaps you're incapacitated. Maybe you are 90 years old and just want your son to step in and help with your finances or come to the doctor with you to make sure your wishes are heard.

We usually create one durable power of attorney for financial matters and one for health care matters. You can name the same folks as your agents, or you can name different people. They can be family members, friends, or professional fiduciaries. Having these documents in place makes things more manageable when you need help, and it can also help you avoid guardianship. If someone obtains guardianship of you, many of your civil rights may be stripped away. That person may be able to decide where you're going to live and take over your finances completely. Most people would rather avoid that. So durable powers of attorney are critical.

We also create health care advance directives for our clients. Suppose you become terminally ill, permanently unconscious, or develop an advanced state of Alzheimer's. In those circumstances, many people say they would not want to be kept alive by artificial means, such as a feeding tube or a mechanical ventilator. My clients tend to feel strongly about whether or not they would want these life-sustaining treatments used in case of terminal illness, for example. Some consider the quality of life that those treatments are likely to provide them and say "no thanks." Others may have religious reasons for wanting certain treatments. Either way, having an advance directive in place lets them make their wishes known.

What is probate?

Sharon Rutberg: Probate comes from the Latin term "to prove." If someone dies with a will, the will can be taken into court, and the judge can be asked to declare the will valid. More broadly, probate is a legal process designed to provide an orderly way to settle the estate of someone who has died. This includes collecting and preserving the deceased person's assets, paying their bills, doing their taxes, and finally distributing the assets. If there is a valid will, the assets may be distributed according to the person's wishes stated in the will. Some assets may pass according to beneficiary designations instead -- retirement accounts often work that way, for example.

Probate gets a bad rap. In some states where probate is particularly expensive, that reputation may be justified. In our state of Washington, we often tell people not to fear probate. In most circumstances, there are laws designed to keep the probate costs down, and the probate process can provide some protection to the estate and its beneficiaries.

In many states, though, it's very popular to use revocable living trusts to avoid the need for probate. You still need a will, called a "pour-over will," but it just says that all of your assets get poured into the trust if you die.

Preferably, however, everything is already in the trust. So instead of a couple owning their house, the trust owns the house, and bank accounts are in the name of the trust. According to the trust rules, the trustee settles the estate when the person who set up the trust (called the trustor or settlor) dies. The trustee may be able to avoid going to court altogether, minimizing legal fees and otherwise keeping the costs down.

Even in Washington, a revocable trust can be very helpful. For example, suppose you own vacation properties in multiple states when you die. In that case, your family could be looking at opening what we call ancillary probate in all those states, which could mean more lawyers and more complications. So having all those properties owned by one trust could be a great solution.

However, a problem arises when a couple pays several thousand dollars to set up a revocable living trust and then fails to put their assets into it. If the trust does not own their home and accounts and boat and other assets, their estate may still need to be probated. And there are times when it's not beneficial to have assets in a revocable trust. For example, in our state, having your house in this type of trust may interfere with Medicaid planning.

Generally, there is no one cookie-cutter solution. We look at each client's needs and create a custom estate planning solution for them. And that's what a good estate lawyer should do.

What inspired you to get started in elder law and estate planning?

Sharon Rutberg: I've been a lawyer for a long time. I graduated from Northwestern Law School in 1988. I worked in Washington, DC, for quite a while. I was at a big firm, worked at the State Department, and did a short stint in the Clinton White House. I took a couple of years off when my children were born to focus on them and reassess my career. Then my family moved to California for my husband's job and then again up to Seattle just because we liked it.

When I returned to practicing law, I really wanted to focus on working with families and individuals. I went through about five difficult years in my late 20s and early 30s trying to help my mother, who was very sick. So I have a lot of compassion for families dealing with older relatives who are declining. It's a terribly emotional and challenging time. I thought it would be rewarding to work with those families. And I think the intricacies of writing wills and trusts and thinking about how these documents all work together is fascinating.

> ### *How can people connect with you and learn more?*

Sharon Rutberg: Our firm in Seattle is Salmon Bay Law Group, PLLC. Our website has more information -- www.salmonbaylaw.com. There is also a lot of great information about elder law legal services, including an attorney locator, on the National Academy of Elder Law Attorneys website, www.naela.org. Many states also have their own chapters - in Washington, ours is called WAELA, www.waela.org.

SHARON C. RUTBERG

Attorney
Salmon Bay Law Group

Sharon Rutberg opened her neighborhood law practice in 2014 to assist individuals and families with estate planning, probate, and elder law matters. She enjoys helping her clients find the peace of mind that comes from getting their important legal concerns addressed.

Sharon is a member of the Real Property, Probate & Trust (RPPT) Sections of the Washington State Bar Association and King County Bar Association, and a former Editor of the Washington Bar's RPPT Newsletter. She belongs to the National Academy of Elder Law Attorneys (NAELA) and serves on the Board of the Washington Academy of Elder Law Attorneys (WAELA).

Sharon received an LL.M. (Master of Laws) degree in Elder Law at the Seattle University School of Law. As an elder law attorney, Sharon works with seniors on estate planning and issues relating to long-term care, including Medicaid planning. Sharon also works with the families of disabled children and adults to set up special needs trusts.

Sharon graduated from Swarthmore College with honors and Northwestern University School of Law, where she served on the Law Review and received the Order of the Coif (top 10%) cum laude. She practiced corporate and government law in Washington, D.C., before heading west to Seattle and redirecting her practice to serving individuals and families. As a D.C. lawyer, Sharon worked for Wilmer, Cutler & Pickering (now WilmerHale), the U.S. State Department, and the Office of the White House Counsel.

Sharon enjoys walking her dogs, reading, and spending time with her husband and two adult children when she is not practicing law.

WEBSITE:
www.salmonbaylaw.com

PHONE:
206-735-3177, ext. 2

EMAIL:
sharon@salmonbaylaw.com

TED ALATSAS

Ted Alatsas

CONVERSATION WITH TED ALATSAS

> *Ted, you are an attorney and founder of Alatsas Law Firm in Brooklyn, New York. Tell us about your practice and the people you help.*

Ted Alatsas: Our firm's mission statement is to preserve our client's assets, provide them help, and protect their future. At Alatsas Law, we provide the one-on-one guidance you need when you're struggling to resolve an elder law or asset protection issue. We explain complex legal concepts in easy-to-understand terms and encourage all of our clients to fully participate in the decision-making process so they can face their future with confidence.

What are the consequences of not planning?

Ted Alatsas: Generally speaking, we find that people aren't as prepared as they should be. I think people tend to neglect to protect their assets. They're good at focusing on trying to accumulate them. They put away money for their retirement, scrimp and save throughout a lifetime, and make hard choices and sacrifices so that they have a sizable nest egg for their golden years. People are savvy enough to maximize their pensions, contributions to 401Ks, IRAs, and other investments, but when it comes to planning where everything is supposed to go when they're gone, they tend to be more willing to let that all to chance. Eventually, they run into a scenario where they panic at the last minute, trying to protect their assets because of a medical concern or unsure where they want it all to go. We try to focus our clients on identifying their needs, articulating their intentions, and ensuring that those intentions suit their needs. And it doesn't cost a whole lot to do. The downside of not doing anything is undoubtedly worse than the cost of doing something.

There are many different things to consider. The first concern is what would happen if you were to get sick and go into a nursing home? If you haven't planned your estate properly, then the nursing home will take everything you've got. For example, in New York City, it costs about $14,000 a month for the average nursing home stay. But, on the other hand, if you properly plan your estate and take advantage of the "five-year look back," you can avoid having to pay out of your pocket, qualify for Medicaid coverage, preserve the legacy you have, and make sure it goes to your kids. It doesn't make much sense to work for 30 years, sacrifice to accumulate a house and a pension, and then let it all go to the government because you get sick. There's no reason why you can't plan for that.

The second concern is that if you haven't planned your estate and you don't have a will in place, the courts can then determine what will happen to your assets when you're gone. This is called intestacy, and basically, that means that a predetermined statutory framework that disregards your particular family says who gets your assets when you're gone. It also means countless delays and costs. Unless you have a complete disregard for that, there is no reason you can't make a reasonable investment to plan accordingly.

What is power of attorney?

Ted Alatsas: If you become incapacitated, you will want someone to make decisions on your behalf. These people have to be assigned ahead of time while you are still of sound mind and able to express your wishes and execute documents. People often come to me when it is already too late. At that point, they are kind of stuck in limbo. It is essential to designate an agent to manage your affairs when you are still healthy. If you have strong feelings about resuscitation or other extreme medical measures, putting these wishes in writing will put your family and yourself at ease.

What is the first step for a new client wanting your help?

Ted Alatsas: We recommend that people come in for an initial strategy session to look at the whole picture. What have you accumulated over your lifetime? What are your family dynamics? What are your goals and objectives? When we put all of those factors together, we make specific recommendations about services we can provide to help reach those goals. It doesn't work very well if you don't have a goal in mind or a sense of how you want things to go. So it's important to have that focus when you come in to see us. If a client comes in without that focus, we outline the ramifications of doing nothing and help them create a plan.

What inspired you to get started in elder law and estate planning?

Ted Alatsas: I'm a product of my community. I grew up in the Sheepshead Bay neighborhood of Brooklyn, and my office continues to be in that same neighborhood. When I was a little kid, I was helping seniors and immigrant families fill out and understand complicated documents and papers. As the son of Greek immigrants in a neighborhood with many Greek members, I was always one of those people who would help others translate documents and understand how to fill out forms. So from a young age, my interest was in helping people. It was a natural progression for me to go into the practice of law, and then eventually into the areas of elder law and estate planning because that is, I believe, one of the areas where I get to help people the most in terms of planning their legacies and protecting their assets. So it's very fulfilling for me as an attorney. It is rewarding to help people with things they can feel on a personal level.

> ### *How can people connect with you and learn more?*

Ted Alatsas: We have many different resources available to anyone looking to reach out. You can call us directly at 718-233-2903 or visit our website at www.alatsaslaw-firm.com. In addition, we have lots of free guides for people to download, and you can make an appointment with us to learn more about our services.

TED ALATSAS

Attorney, Founder
Alatsas Law Firm

Theodore Alatsas, Esq. is the founder of the Alatsas Law Firm and the developer of the firm's 3 Pillars of Protection - our mission to Preserve your assets,

Provide you Help, and Protect your Future focusing in three separate and related areas of law - Divorce and Family, Elder Law & Estate Planning, and Consumer Bankruptcy.

Born the child of Greek immigrants in the early 1970s, Theodore Alatsas, Esq. grew up in Sheepshead Bay, Brooklyn. Theodore learned the importance of hard work and dedication to his community at an early age, working his way through high school and college in his parents' deli. As an exemplary student and community activist, Theodore often volunteered his time to help those who needed it. Theodore attended Brooklyn Technical High School, New York University on a scholarship and St. John's University School of Law.

Theodore's work in the areas of Divorce and Family Law, Elder Law and Estate Planning, and Consumer Bankruptcy Law have earned him recognition from several professional organizations, including the Lawyers of Distinction, The American Institute of Family Law Attorneys, Attorney and Practice Magazine, Martindale Hubbell, and Avvo, as well as dozens of 5-star reviews from past clients. As an active member of the legal community, Theodore continues to influence changes in the practice of law. He serves on a number of professional boards as a member of the New York State Bar Association, The Brooklyn Bar Association, The New

York City Bar Association, The Hellenic American Bar Association, The American Bankruptcy Institute, the National Association of Consumer Bankruptcy Attorneys, The National Academy of Elder Law Attorneys, and the National Association of Divorce Professionals.

As a Certified Divorce Specialist by the N.A.D.P., Theodore has earned recognition for exemplifying professionalism in working with divorce and family law clients, having handled matters ranging from straightforward uncontested divorce to complicated trials. In each case, Theodore Alatsas and his team strive to provide their clients with the kind of representation that empowers them to preserve their assets, provide them help and protect their future.

In the areas of Elder Law and Estate Planning, Theodore demonstrated his expertise in 2019, having co-authored the New York edition of "Medicaid Secrets: How to Protect Your Family's Assets from Devastating Nursing Home Costs" and is currently working on the soon to be released 2021 edition. An active member of the National Academy of Elder Law Attorneys and the New York State Bar Association's Elder Law, Trusts and Estates committee, Theodore remains active in the development and discussion of new laws and changes to existing procedures to keep his clients' estate plans up to date and their assets protected.

Growing up in the community, Theodore witnessed firsthand the challenges hard-working people often face when the economy turns or when unexpected medical bills devastate a family. To help clients in their deepest need, Theodore has focused his third pillar of protection on consumer bankruptcy. Whether handling a Chapter 7 matter or working to preserve a client's home in a Chapter 13, Theodore and his team have developed a personalized approach to managing clients through the complicated web of the bankruptcy code to help them get the fresh start they deserve.

During his early 20s, Theodore worked his way through college and law school while at the same time actively participating and leading various civic organizations. Among these organizations are the Avenue U Merchants' Association, Citizens for Neighborhood Action, Change NY, and the Joint Council of Kings County Boards of Trade. Theodore's community involvement was recognized in New York Newsday, the Bay News, and various other community papers.

After graduating from law school, Theodore began the practice of law in the same location where his parents owned a Greek deli. Over the years, his practice areas have become more specialized to focus primarily on divorce and family law. His knowledge and experience as a neighborhood practitioner have uniquely qualified him to handle a matter not only from a legal perspective but with compassion designed to guide the client through the process as smoothly as possible.

Theodore remains active in his community and has been nominated as a candidate for various public offices, including Brooklyn District Attorney and Brooklyn Borough President, and served as a member of the Public Service Commission Siting Board after having been appointed to the position by Governor Pataki in 2002.

Theodore continues to reside in Brooklyn with his wife and daughter, and his law firm is located on the very spot he was raised. He is fluent in Greek and Spanish.

WEBSITE:
www.alatsaslawfirm.com

PHONE:
718-233-2903

EMAIL:
ted@alatsaslaw.com

FACEBOOK:
https://www.facebook.com/TedAlatsasEsq/

LINKEDIN:
https://www.linkedin.com/in/theodore-alatsas-7361275/

ABOUT THE PUBLISHER

Mark Imperial is a Best-Selling Author, Syndicated Business Columnist, Syndicated Radio Host, and internationally recognized Stage, Screen, and Radio Host of numerous business shows spotlighting leading experts, entrepreneurs, and business celebrities.

His passion is to discover noteworthy business owners, professionals, experts, and leaders who do great work and share their stories and secrets to their success with the world on his syndicated radio program titled "Remarkable Radio."

Mark is also the media marketing strategist and voice for some of the world's most famous brands. You can hear his voice over the airwaves weekly on Chicago radio and worldwide on iHeart Radio.

Mark is a Karate black belt; teaches Muay Thai and Kickboxing; loves Thai food, House Music, and his favorite TV shows are infomercials.

Learn more:

www.MarkImperial.com
www.BooksGrowBusiness.com

Made in the USA
Columbia, SC
21 October 2021